IMAGES OF ENGLAND

BELLE VUE

IMAGES OF ENGLAND

BELLE VUE

JILL CRONIN AND FRANK RHODES

TEMPUS

In memory of Stan Horritt

Frontispiece: A publicity stunt outside Manchester town hall to
advertise Belle Vue Zoo in August 1964. The Albert Memorial,
in front of the town hall, is reflected in both hub caps of the car.
John Jennison, Belle Vue's first owner, had been adept at publicising
his pleasure gardens. So too were the subsequent managers the
Iles through the 1940s and 1950s. Gerald Iles, in particular, as zoo
director, did much to advertise his zoo, by the use of publicity stunts,
celebrity names for new animals and broadcasting on Children's
Hour. Belle Vue had been called 'the showground of the world'.

First published 1999, reprinted 2001, 2005

Tempus Publishing Limited
The Mill, Brimscombe Port,
Stroud, Gloucestershire, GL5 2QG
www.tempus-publishing.com

British Library Cataloguing in Publication Data.
A catalogue record for this book is available from the British Library.

ISBN 0 7524 1571 9

Typesetting and origination by Tempus Publishing Limited.
Printed in Great Britain.

Contents

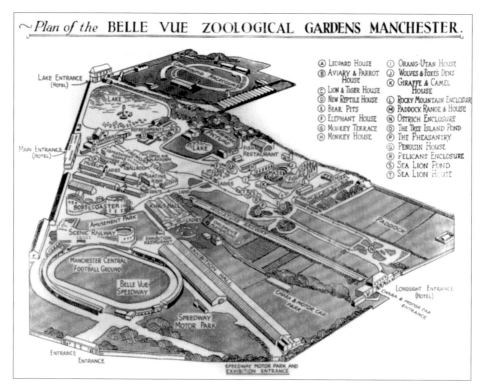

Plan of Belle Vue taken from the official guide book of 1931. The first guide book was produced in 1847 and so the development of the site can be traced over the years. In the pre-Second World War period, the gardens were very successful under the management of John Henry Iles. All three entrances were in operation. The zoo and amusement park were both expanding and were complemented by the two lakes, firework displays, stadiums for greyhound racing and for speedway and exhibition sites. Refreshment areas were plentiful.

Introduction

Signposts still point the way to Belle Vue in Gorton but the visitor arrives at a sprawling area of car auction rooms, housing estates and a cinema complex. It is hard to imagine 'the beautiful view' once conjured up by the name Belle Vue and yet, for over 140 years, here lay one of the early pleasure gardens of England, a theme park, which ironically closed just before theme parks became so popular again.

The year 1818 saw the construction of the new Hyde Road across the marshy, open land at Belle Vue, providing a new route into Manchester. In 1804 the Collegiate church of Manchester had leased lands in Kirkmanshulme to John Gill of Heaton Norris and it is likely that in about 1820 it was he that built an inn-cum-farm house on this new road, known as Belle Vue House, with stables, gardens and a bowling green. These premises were in turn leased to John Jennison in 1836 who opened 'Belle Vue Gardens' incorporating his small zoo transferred from the 'Strawberry Gardens' at Adswood. He swiftly acquired more land for expansion, including, in 1843, 13 acres of adjacent farmland and by 1905 Belle Vue consisted of no less than 68 acres of land inside and 97 acres outside its walls. From 1850 the name 'Belle Vue' had also become associated with the Belle Vue prison, which lay at the Manchester end of Belle Vue's site.

Jennison was innovative and bold and the gardens became a major attraction for not only Manchester people but hordes of visitors for miles around. His beautiful gardens were laid out with attention to detail and, like his animal houses, were designed in elaborate themes. An Indian-style temple housed the monkeys and an outdoor Indian grotto the reptiles. There were Italian and Chinese gardens, two lakes, glasshouses, a maze and a tree-lined avenue. Catering was important and themed cafés and bars were introduced, such as the Chinese and Pagoda Restaurants, the Lighthouse and Maze Cafés and the Jolly Buffet Bar. Later steam-driven rides formed the embryo of an amusement park with a horse ride, the Velocipedes and the Ocean Wave.

Dancing and music were everywhere with bands playing indoors and out and with an outdoor wooden dance floor, as well as the huge Music Hall, soon to become the Great Ballroom. Jennison had not finished yet! He invited brass bands to compete at Belle Vue, in what became a premier annual competition. He introduced gigantic, annual firework displays, set on an island in the lake with a huge 'painted picture' as a backdrop to a battle scene, enacted by hordes of people and sometimes animals as well.

Families, parties and firms were all encouraged to come to Belle Vue for celebrations, special meals and events. The Jennisons were an almost self-sufficient entity with their own brewery, nursery gardens, brickworks and printing, scenery and firework workshops. Outside and inside the walls they had houses for their employees and public houses for their visitors.

Jennison exploited the developing transport systems to get people to the site. The three entrances were served by four railway stations, regularly served by special excursion trains and there were large stabling blocks for horses. Later he created huge parking areas to accommodate charabancs and finally buses and cars. Jennison ran Belle Vue with the help of his large family and when he died in 1869 they continued his work and Belle Vue's growth. From the 1890s until the 1920s the gardens were probably at their peak of popularity. The years after the First World War saw a decline and in 1925 the family sold out to a new company, Belle Vue (Manchester) Ltd.

John Henry Iles headed this company until 1937, ably helped by members of his family. His brother, William, initially, ran the zoo but his son, Gerald, was zoo director from 1933 until 1957. His ideas and enthusiasm made the zoo's name a respected one worldwide. John Henry's son, H.F.B. Iles, took over from his father as chairman until 1970. There were some major additions, during the early years of this company, including an annual Christmas circus from 1929, the country's first greyhound racing stadium opened in 1926 and the first purpose-built speedway stadium in 1929. During wartime Belle Vue played its part. The military took over large areas of the grounds and aircraft parts and munitions were produced there. Dinners were given for soldiers and children and entertainment provided for the war weary public. Many of the employees enlisted and after the war a memorial was erected in Gorton cemetery for those who were lost.

From 1945 until the early 1950s there was a brief post-war boom at Belle Vue, as people began to enjoy themselves again. Taxes, however, were high and money was short and the long, slow decline in Belle Vue's fortunes began. In 1956 Sir Leslie Joseph and Charles Forte bought Belle Vue, retaining Gerald Iles as zoo director and H.F.B. Iles as chairman. The Forte family enhanced the catering facilities, developing banqueting facilities, such as the Cumberland, Windermere and Kendal suites and adding the Exhibition Hall. By 1963 Charles Forte was in sole control and there was a boom, especially in catering, and the future was looking rosier.

In the early 1960s Belle Vue could still attract 150,000 people on an Easter Monday but by 1968 the visitor figures for Bank Holidays had dropped to around 30,000. Competition from other theme and amusement parks were now having an effect. In the 1970s the once popular catering attractions were now seeing a decline and so was dancing. The speedway, circus and exhibition halls still flourished for while but a final turning point was reached when Belle Vue lost its bid to become Manchester's new exhibition centre. The zoo became run down and closed in 1977. The amusement park continued to be run by franchises for a while but despite several efforts made by local groups to save Belle Vue, rising costs, vandalism and numerous fires took their toll. In 1981 most of the site was sold for housing and industrial use although the First Leisure group bought the bowling and leisure interests. Granada Bowl eventually became a bingo hall. Of the 68 acres that were once Belle Vue Gardens, the greatest attraction in the North, only the greyhound stadium and snooker hall survive today.

Many of the photographs from which this book is composed come from the collection of the late Stan Horritt with additions provided by Allan Crockford and the archive at Chetham's Library. Each chapter has a theme that follows the development and decline in turn of the grounds, the zoo, the circus, musical activities, the amusement rides, special events and celebrity visits. Many of the people involved in running the spectacle that was Belle Vue over its long career are illustrated here along with just a few of the millions who were its visitors over the years.

John Jennison achieved a good deal and certainly fulfilled his mottoes: 'Do it yourself' and 'Novelty, always novelty'. In 1932 the *Daily Herald* summed up Belle Vue's recipe for success: 'the secret of Belle Vue is this, that it represents Lancashire's own ideal of an amusement sort, built up slowly piece by piece and feature by feature over nearly a century. Originally here was a farm, where Belle Vue now stands, with a small wayside inn, to which people would jog along on horseback or walk, to pass a homely evening. From this, step by step, has grown up the huge 70 acres city we know today, which attracts over 2,000,000 visitors every year, and where it takes a clever man to think of a diversion he will not find tucked away somewhere.'

One

The Way In and
the Grounds

A crowd of children make their way into Belle Vue in April 1946, on their way to the Hallé Orchestra's parry for schoolchildren. From 1942 and for thirty years the Hallé had its home at Belle Vue (see p. 36). Belle Vue hosted many parties during and just after the war for children, evacuees and wounded soldiers (see pp 85-87). It was well equipped to do so with its suites of banqueting halls.

Above: An early view of Hyde Road taken from the entrance to Belle Vue gardens, painted by George Danson. The lane on the right later became Belle Vue Street. The site was originally home to the Belle Vue house, an inn and farmhouse. In 1852 George and his sons came from London to Belle Vue as scenic designers and painters. They were responsible for the colourful backdrops to the fireworks displays (see pp 98-100). In 1947 this painting was acquired by Manchester City Art Gallery.

Opposite: John Jennison Snr, on the right, with some of his family in the Ornamental Gardens at Belle Vue. Jennison was the inspiration and founder of Belle Vue pleasure gardens, which he ran, helped by his numerous sons, from 1836 until his death in 1869, aged seventy-nine. His tomb is in Cheadle graveyard. His sons continued to run the gardens until 1925, when Belle Vue (Manchester) Ltd, headed by John Henry Iles, took over. The gardens became part of the Forte empire in the 1950s and eventually closed in 1981.

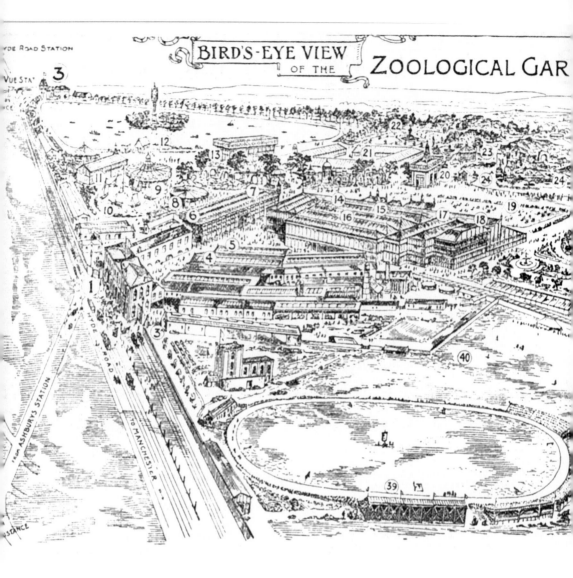

A bird's-eye view of Belle Vue engraved in 1895 and in use in the guidebooks until 1925. This three-dimensional drawing complements the plans of 1931 and 1892 by bringing them to life. Many of Jennison's elegant buildings of the 1850s are still in use here and the layout of the gardens, lakes and

BELLEVUE MANCHESTER.

sports areas can be appreciated. The site, originally comprising about 36 acres in 1836 had increased to 68 acres inside the walls by 1905. This plan gradually became obsolete, as buildings were replaced and new features were added.

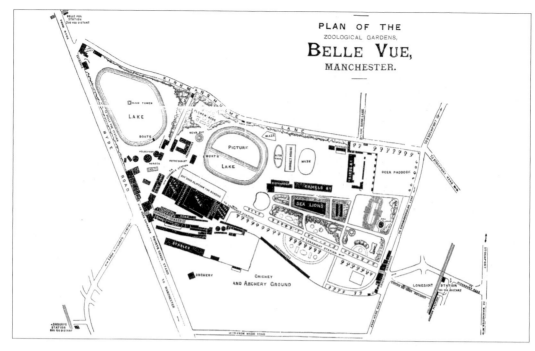

PLAN OF THE
ZOOLOGICAL GARDENS,
BELLE VUE,
MANCHESTER.

A plan of Belle Vue published in the 1892 penny guide to the zoological gardens. It is interesting to compare this with the plan of 1931 seen earlier to see how the site grew and changed. Plans were added to each guidebook from 1881. This one shows a more sedate site with tea-rooms, animal houses and steam horses set out in beautifully landscaped gardens. The amusement park, athletics ground and greyhound and speedway stadiums were yet to come. The large chara' and motor park shown on the 1931 plan was not yet needed but visitors could leave their horses and carriages free of charge in long rows of stables near the Hyde Road and lake entrances.

'Buckland' (D. Buckland-Smith), press and publicity chief at Belle Vue from 1945-1956. John Jennison had always courted publicity for his gardens and set up in 1856 his own printing office, 'where the placards and handbills are printed announcing the extra attractions of the gardens etc. Beneath the printing room are dens for animals...'. He could thus print his own guidebooks too. This office closed in 1929 but in the 1950s a Belle Vue newsheet was started. Buckland headed the publicity at Belle Vue and became a well-known figure, promoting it by his own force of character and skill. His was the film proclaiming Belle Vue as 'the showground of the world'.

The main entrance to Belle Vue in the early 1950s showing the Palm Court Bar on the left and the 'Bobs' on the right. 'The Hyde Road entrance, which is the most central, is on the north side of the gardens, on the Hyde road, and is approached from Manchester, either by that road, or by the Ashton Road.' This impressive two-storied entrance was built in 1850. The Natural History Museum was moved from Firework Island in 1856 to the upper floor near here and was reached by a spiral staircase. Downstairs was an aviary, soon to be replaced by 'wild beasts'. In 1873 the entrance was enlarged and by 1956 the distinctive blue and yellow turnstiles were in place.

The Longsight entrance in 1907. 'The Longsight, or Western entrance, is near the Longsight station, on the London and North-Western railway. Omnibuses and tramcars also run from Market Street every three minutes during the day to this entrance It is used chiefly by visitors from the southernmost parts of the city...' John Jennsion was quick to utilise the chance of railway excursions. The Hyde Road entrance was used by rail visitors from Hyde Road station from 1855 and Longsight station had opened in 1842. 'Ashbury's for Belle Vue' was opened in 1875 and then a new eastern or Gorton entrance was added in 1876 at the lake end of the site to cater for visitors arriving at the new Belle Vue station.

The Longsight entrance on Redgate Lane, west of Hunter's Lane, prior to demolition in 1985. When built in 1851 at a cost of £1,000, this entrance was an impressive structure with a ballroom in its upper storey. Accommodating 500 dancers, the ballroom was run by Mr and Mrs Arthur Wantling, who invented the Lola tango. They moved out when the roof began to leak. The ballroom was demolished in the 1950s.

The turnstiles at the Hyde Road entrance to Belle Vue in the early 1970s. The posters advertise the range of attractions available. This gate had seen crowds of hundreds in the gardens' heyday and each photograph of them is now a fashion plate of the times, as everybody would be in 'Sunday Best' for a visit to Belle Vue. In 1846 it cost 4d to get in and a family season ticket was 10s or 5s for a single. Rail excursions brought in thousands each year from 1847 until the mid-1960s. In the 1930s there were seven huge parking areas for charabancs and motor cars. The zoo was the oldest in the United Kingdom after those at London and Bristol.

An advertisement for Belle Vue, 1948.

A view of the grounds with the First Class café to the left, originally the Elephant House. The circular area in the middle later became the hippopotamus pool. The grounds were enhanced with long tree-lined avenues from 1853 onwards, linking the Longsight entrance with the station and with Kirkmanshulme Lane and later leading from the Hyde Road entrance. In the early 1930s 'the gardens with pleasant walks, fountains and shrubberies were still much as they were when John Jennison himself walked them with his top hat, flowered waistcoat and tall cane.'

The cover to the 1899 official guidebook to Belle Vue. This booklet cost 1d and contained over thirty pages of detailed descriptions for each type of animal, amusement and facility in the gardens, set out as a guided tour. The cover depicted the most popular animals with the monkeys represented by their house in the top right of the left-hand side. On the bottom left is the Great Lake with its clock tower island. This cover was printed in brilliant colours.

The Italian Garden

Above: The Italian Gardens at Belle Vue, in about 1900, laid out in 1870 by George Jennison. The Tropical Plant House is in the background. 'Afterwards they had the snakes outside in a garden in a pit, the Italian Garden.' In the late 1800s 'the resort relied almost entirely for its attraction on its delightful gardens … Belle Vue could boast conservatories, formal gardens and billiard-table lawns, such as could be seen nowhere else in Lancashire.' By 1931, however, 'formalism, keep hothouse delicacy have gone. Everywhere are flowers and plants; in the open gardens, in the covered halls. Everywhere is cool, restful green; lawns, edgings, trees. Everywhere, too, are comfortable benches and rustic seats where visitors can rest, enjoy sun or shade as they desire, keep an eye on this or that entertainment, read or even indulge in a restful doze.'

Left: Leonard Williams at Belle Vue in the 1920s. 'My dad grew all the flowers for Belle Vue, for the beds and the clock they had at the front. They grew loads of flowers for the Reptile House, the cafés, restaurants and ballrooms. My dad was in charge of the gardens at Belle Vue for nineteen years. He was ninety-six when he died.'

Right: Leonard Williams in a greenhouse at Belle Vue in the 1920s. 'My dad had one or two working for him. The potting shed, a long, narrow shed, was where the public was not allowed. I used to take his lunch sometimes. I can still smell the potting shed, where Dad did the flowers, the hothouse where he grew *Hoya carnosa*, which is still my favourite flower. When a snake escaped, a small snake, they couldn't find it and they looked all over for it and it was missing quite a while. One day, my dad was in the greenhouse showing people round and a woman said, "Ooh, there's a little bird up there, right up above, in a little hole" and he knew right way, my dad, what it was. It was the snake and it was up there.'

Below: The Indian temple and grotto in about 1900. In 1886 a monkey house was built in an Indian style and in 1898 rustic grottoes were set out as a ruined Indian temple, designed by George Danson, Belle Vue's scenic artist. 'Inside it was done out like caves out of imitation rock, like a grotto. They used to have the snakes where the flowers were in this grotto thing; they were in 'ere; you just went in. They had a pool there with the crocodiles in. There weren't many of 'em.' By 1903 the Camellia and Orange House had been used as a Reptile House, beginning the long connection between reptiles and flowers at Belle Vue.

Indian Temple & Grotto

Two

On the Water

The Great, later New, Lake and clock tower island at Belle Vue in the early 1900s. 'This eight- acre lake was made [in 1858] by digging out the clay, which was then made into bricks in the zoo's brickworks and used to build the high [perimeter] wall, approximately 13 feet in height,' clearly visible here. The lake lay in the triangular corner of the gardens between Hyde Road and Kirkmanshulme Lane near the lake entrance. The Lake Hotel, visible across the lake, was opened in 1876 with stabling for visitors' horses. Extended and upgraded several times, it was finally closed in the 1980s. Gorton town hall, which opened earlier in 1865, has been omitted — artistic licence!

Another view of the Great Lake, after 1876. Two paddle steamers were in operation by 1862, called the *Little Eastern* and the *Little Britain*. The former was built at Liverpool for service on the Mersey and the latter was said to have been built originally by the government for service in India. The rides were 1d a session, paid at the landing stage paybox and about 100 passengers could be accommodated on each steamer. The clock tower in the centre of the lake came from Alexandra Park in Manchester and was installed by 1882. It served to time the half-hour sessions on the rowing boats. To the right of the Lake Hotel Gorton town hall is this time depicted.

Crowds in front of the Small or Firework Lake in about 1900. This smaller lake was dug out in 1843. On the left is the Lighthouse Café, catering from 1862 until 1977. On the lake can be glimpsed three boats, of which one was named *Favourite*, probably the nearest one in this view, a paddle steamer with sails and with smoke coming out of the funnel. Beyond the boats lies the central island, which was first home to a small natural history museum, which was moved to the upper storey of the main entrance in 1856. Then the island became the backdrop for the firework spectacles, housing the 'Painted Picture', which the steam launches carried visitors over to view.

The Ocean Wave, in place from 1894 in the Jennison amusement area, to the left of the Hyde Road entrance. 'A circular platform, equipped like the bridge of a ship, is set among scenery painted to represent the waves of an ocean during a high wind. Round the edge of the platform is a line of small yachts. Powerful machinery makes the platform revolve, and at the same time rise and fall, giving the yachts a motion not unlike the ones they have at sea.' The Ocean Wave was removed in the early 1930s.

Boating on the Firework Lake in about 1910. The rocks and backdrop of the 'Painted Picture' are clearly visible here. Fishing took place as well and even ice skating. 'One year, when I was about nine, the big lake froze over. It was the only time I remember that and my dad took me skating on there and there was an island in the middle and I skated around that' [about 1929].

Members of the *Show Boat* company enjoying a trip on the Great Lake in about 1930. The Lake Hotel and Gorton town hall are visible in the background. 'Patrons can enjoy a trip in up-to-date motor boats and paddle steamers, or they can indulge in the more arduous task of oarsmanship.' By this time there were 'new motor speed boats, new pedal boats, new blue launches on the Firework Lake. Out-board motor boat racing is a new sport.'

Miniature motor boats on the Firework Lake in the 1930s. The Elephant House and First Class Café are in the background and on the left is the backdrop for the spectacles on Firework Island. In 1858 there were thirty pleasure boats on the two lakes. By 1892 the Great Lake 'has recently been considerably enlarged. Numerous pleasure boats and miniature steamers ply upon this lake; the pleasure boats are let out at the rate of 3d or 4d per half-hour for each passenger and 1d or 2d each is charged for a tour round the lake on the steamers.'

The miniature boats on the Firework or Small Lake in the 1950s, with the Lighthouse Café in the background. By this time things were changing. Although boating continued until 1977 on the Firework Lake, the steamer the *Little Britain*, which plied the Great Lake, was broken up in 1950. In 1956 part of the Great Lake was filled in to make a car park and in 1963 it was finally drained to provide a site for Granada Bowling.

The Waterchute at Belle Vue in August 1964. This ride lay between the ballroom and the 'Bobs' near the Hyde Road entrance. The original waterchute was a far more primitive affair with a man pulling it round and using a flat, wooden boat. In 1956/7 the new Waterchute seen here was opened on the site of the Centenary Gardens. By 1978 it was no longer in use and was later dismantled and transferred to Blackpool's Pleasure Beach.

A publicity photograph for the Waterchute in June 1957. There are various pictures of people in the water near the cars around this time; some of these apparently show people testing new waterproof products!

David Metcalfe and Anne McNamara trying for a record number of rides on the Waterchute in September 1974. In 1978, the Revd Peter Schofield from Hulme went on to break the world record by staying on for forty-one hours to raise money for charity. His boat carried the Union Jack emblem and he wore a blue waterproof jacket that was being tested for a manufacturer. He spent two nights on the ride, going round about 800 times.

Three

Dancing and Music

The ballroom at Belle Vue in the early 1900s. The original Music Hall was built all of wood in 1856 and held 10,000 people on its 27,000 square feet of dance floor. It lay under the firework viewing stand. In 1858 it was extended and George Danson painted frescoes on its panelled ceilings, including the five previous firework pictures. In 1889 it was redecorated in Empire style, renamed the Great Ballroom and gained wall paintings by Caney and mirrored octagonal pillars. In 1928, 'Jennison's original ballroom was there, now serving as the printing shop; the second ballroom was the Natural History Museum. The third great ballroom, with its mirrored pillars and scenic paintings, was a relic of bygone days and fashions.'

The ballroom in the early 1900s, after the 1889 redecoration. The orchestra is seated up above in the balcony at the far end of the ballroom. In the 1930s, there was a 'Grand Ballroom with a splendid floor capable of accommodating 2,500 dancers.' 'We used to play there as a kid, me and my brother. Sunday mornings we used to go through the ballroom and see if there was anything left, before they cleared up. Sometimes we found a few coppers, picture cards or cigarette cards. My dad [head gardener] never knew.'

The open-air dancing platform in the early 1900s. 'A novel feature was the huge outdoor dancing platform laid down between the Firework Lake and grandstand. Here on fine days during the season, thousands of visitors danced to the Belle Vue Military band.' The lake with its 'Painted Picture' is on the right and the Lighthouse Café is centre background, with the Indian Grotto next to it on the left. 'Rope' dancing had been tried in 1845 but this wooden floor was opened in 1852 on the bowling green site. It was extended to half an acre by 1855.

Open-air dancing in the 1920s with the Firework Island behind and the Lighthouse Café on the left. There is at least one soldier in the picture. In 1931 it was described as an 'open-air dancing floor, where dancing takes place throughout the summer'. Various military and brass bands played there, including the Belle Vue Military, the Cyril Mellor, the Arabesque, the Belle Vue Quadrille and the Chetham Hill brass bands. The bandstand could be rotated to face either direction and had a forty foot-high roof and coloured statues of Canova's dancing girls.

The open-air dancing area in the 1930s. Here the view is taken from the Firework Lake side, facing the firework viewing stand. The amusement park is signposted right, in the distance. These wooden boards became slippery in wet weather and were used later as a roller-skating rink. After the Second World War the dance floor was little used and then was destroyed by fire in 1958, together with the Great Ballroom.

Fred Bonelli was leader of the orchestra at Belle Vue from 1928 until his death in 1968: 'But when it comes to selecting music and planning it, Belle Vue's Musical Director, Fred Bonelli is the ideal man for the job. Circus enthusiasts know him mainly for his work in the King's Hall [Christmas Circus]. He plays regularly in our magnificent New Elizabethan ballroom and provides a variety of sound for a variety of reasons throughout this vast showground.'

The Coronation Ballroom in April 1948. In 1937 the ballroom had been refurbished and refloored at a cost of £10,000. It was renamed the Coronation in honour of George VI. The Tudor Restaurant (see pp 83-84) was opened to service it. The band, under the direction of Fred Bonelli, was moved down to the stage area.

'Let's Dance'
after the Circus
in the

New Elizabethan Ballroom

Dancing Nightly
at 7 p.m.

Your Host:
Sam Mason

Monday, Wednesday & Friday -
Ballroom Dancing

Tuesday & Thursday -
Old Tyme Nights
to Bonelli's Orchestra

M.C. Minnie & Harry Green

"BIG NIGHT OUT"
SATURDAYS
Bands — Groups
Two Ballrooms
Top Disc Session
Resident D.J.

Fully Licensed · Special transfer prices

Above: An advertisement for the New Elizabethan Ballroom in 1966/7. The Coronation Ballroom had been destroyed by fire in 1958 and this huge ballroom complex was built on its site in 1959/60. 'It was such a big ballroom. You start dancing at one end and by the time you got down the other end, you couldn't hear him. Many bands also played there, including those of Joe Loss and Phil Moss, who described Belle Vue as 'fifty places rolled into one'. In 1967 the largest Wurlitzer organ in Europe was installed there at a cost of £8,000.

Right: The Coronation Ballroom in April 1948, with its ornate lighting and gilded columns, seating alongside the dance floor and upstairs on the balcony. Its successor the New Elizabethan 'is unsurpassed in Great Britain for size, comfort and elegance, with accommodation for over 4,000 dancers on two fine maple floors. A revolving stage, coloured fountains, crystal chandeliers, rich carpets and the very latest in modern decor make this ballroom a welcome addition to Manchester's entertainment facilities.'

An advertisement for the Sundays Top Ten Club at Belle Vue in 1966/7. Ballroom dancing began to decline in popularity, as pop groups and disco music took over. Many pop groups visited Belle Vue. From 1962 until 1970, this Top Ten Club operated, with Jimmy Savile as the resident DJ until 1968, also becoming 'DJ of the year'. Sir Jimmy remembers 'the Elizabethan Ballroom was a magic place. Never less than 1,000 dancers (actually jivers) and up to 3,000. Loved by everybody, it was a weekend must for Manchester teens and twenties.' It was 'the largest teenage dance club in the country'. In 1974 it reopened as the Stardust Club.

An advertisement for Danceland in 1975. As interest in ballroom dancing continued to decline in the early 1970s, the New Elizabethan complex added Danceland, with its Crystal Room given over to the 'Zoo-B-Doo' disco. By 1978, popularity for this had also declined and ballroom dancing had ceased to be of interest to almost anyone and the complex closed in 1979.

The massed brass band event at the open championships in the Kings' Hall in the early 1950s. Brass bands had played at Belle Vue for open-air dancing and as entertainment for the crowds at Whitsun. In 1852 John Jennison had experimented with a drum and fife contest. In the following year he held the first of the September brass bands competition, contributing £20 towards the prize fund. No professionals could perform, entry was a £1 deposit per band and they were free to select their own tunes. The contest was attended by 16,000 people and was won by the Mossley Temperance Sax Horn band. In 1886 a second annual contest was introduced in July and later one in May as well. From 1900 the contest was renamed the British Open Brass Band Championship.

BELLE VUE
ZOOLOGICAL GARDENS, MANCHESTER.

Under Rules approved by the N.B.B.C.

The 92nd Annual
SEPTEMBER
CHAMPIONSHIP
BRASS BAND CONTEST
OPEN TO ALL AMATEUR BANDS

in the KINGS HALL,
SATURDAY, SEPT. 2nd, 1944,
Commencing at 12 noon

Promoted by BELLE VUE Manchester LTD

BOARD OF DIRECTORS

J. R. ILES, M.A., J.P. Chairman and Joint Managing Director
E. O. SPENCE Joint Managing Director and Chief Administrator
FREDK. A. SCOTT
W. S. CULLEN, F.C.A.

Secretary: C. M. DIXON, F.C.A.A.

CONTEST MANAGER FRANK PARKER

PROGRAMME . . THREEPENCE

The programme cover for the 92nd Annual September Championship Brass Band Contest in the Kings' Hall, in 1944. From the 1900s until 1929 the contests were held in the ballroom with half the seats reserved and the rest standing room. 'There were no uniforms: they played without waistcoat or coat and with shirt sleeves rolled up. There were now test pieces from famous operas.' In 1912 at the Diamond Jubilee (60th) Contest, the Belle Vue Champion Challenge cup was offered and was won by Foden's Motor Works band. Each member of the winning band received a gold medal with a diamond setting. During the First World War the competition was suspended.

BELLE VUE
ZOOLOGICAL GARDENS, MANCHESTER.

3rd ANNUAL CHAMPIONSHIP

Brass Band Marching Contest
and the

1st GRAND NATIONAL CHAMPIONSHIP

A.T.C. Band Marching Contest
ON THE STADIUM,

Sunday, June 11th, 1944,
at 2-15 p.m.

Compere and Massed Band Conductor
J. HENRY ILES, Esq.

Promoted by BELLE VUE (Manchester) LTD.

BOARD OF DIRECTORS

H. F. B. ILES, M.A. J.P. Chairman and Joint Managing Director
E. O. SPENCE. Joint Managing Director and Chief Administrator
FREDK. A. SCOTT
W. B. CULLEN, F.C.A.

Secretary R. M. DIXON, F.C.R.A.

CONTEST MANAGER FRANK PARKER

PROGRAMME · · THREEPENCE

Printed by Mark Buckley Press Street, Openshaw Manchester —4m 5/6,44

Above: Marching bands at Belle Vue stadium in the early 1950s. Like John Jennison, John Henry Iles, chairman of Belle Vue from 1928, was a fan of brass bands from his first visit in September 1898. He turned the contest into a national event, moulding amateur brass bands into a national movement. He introduced new and original test pieces from 1928. In 1936 he also achieved a massed band performance by 2,700 bandsmen to mark Belle Vue's centenary. From 1942 marching contests were held in the stadium each June.

Left: The programme cover of the Third Annual Championship of the Brass Band Marching Contest, including the First ATC Band Marching Contest, in the stadium in June 1944. John Henry Iles personally compered and conducted the annual massed band concert. He had also set up an Iles Challenge Championship trophy. The Second World War did not stop the contests altogether: 'that strange day in September 1939, when a comparatively small company, laden with gas-masks, assembled to hear nine bands compete between lunch and tea.'

1853 · 1952

The
Centenary

100th ANNIVERSARY OF THE GREAT

September Open Championship Brass Band Contest

★

Held in the Kings Hall, Belle Vue
Manchester, England
on **Saturday, 6th September, 1952**

★

UNDER THE GRACIOUS PATRONAGE
OF HER MAJESTY THE QUEEN

Centenary **Souvenir Programme** *Centenary*
ONE SHILLING & SIXPENCE

The centenary of the September Open Championship Brass Band Contest held in the Kings' Hall in 1952. John's son, Henry F.B. Iles, who followed him as chairman, revived the contest, introducing a new era in 1952. There was a £2,000 gold trophy and a first prize of £150. By 1952 Besses o'Th' Barn had won twenty-three times since 1869, Black Dyke Mills fifteen since 1862, Foden's Motors Works fourteen since 1909 and Fairey Aviation Works had won a prize every September since 1941. In 1954 the Spring Brass Band Contest was inaugurated, amalgamating the May and July competitions.

Above: The 117th annual British Open Brass Band Championship Contest in the Kings' Hall in September 1969. Interest in the contests had waned somewhat for a while but in the early l970s there was a revived popularity but it was a sad day when the last brass band event, the North West Amateur championship, was held in the Kings' Hall in February 1982. Fifty-six bands participated before a crowd of 1,700 and the Dobcross band won first prize.

Left: The programme cover for the Hallé orchestra's performance of *Aida* in the Kings' Hall in 1946. The Hallé came to Belle Vue in 1942, because the Free Trade Hall was blitzed, and played regularly there for over thirty years. John Barbirolli was one of its most famous conductors. A choral competition had been tried in 1903, as well as later hand-bell ringing, concertina and bugle band contests. Gorton Philharmonic Society played at Belle Vue for eighty-nine years, from 1887, and then transferred to Stockport. 'I used to see the Hallé there and the brass bands. They had everything there. I went with my husband when we were courting [Margaret married in 1950] to see the Hallé. I went to see Gigli. I saw a lot of famous people there.'

Four

At the Circus

A small girl admires a pelican as she visits Chipperfield's circus at Belle Vue in the 1970s. The circus came to Belle Vue every Christmas time for about a month. A summer circus was tried but unsuccessfully. Belle Vue International Circus included acts from many countries. Famous circuses such as Chipperfields, the Moscow State and the Hungarian State also visited.

Advertisements for the Coronation Ballroom and for the 20th Belle Vue International Circus, in 1948/49. The first circus was tried at Christmas 1929 in the King's Hall. Zoo director, Gerald Iles' father, William, collaborated with Alderman Tom Bickerstaff of the Blackpool Tower Company and that circus was brought to Belle Vue, together with its ringmaster, George Lockhart.

George Lockhart was ringmaster of Belle Vue Circus from 1929 until 1972. George became 'Uncle George, prince of ringmasters and star of ringmasters'. He had full authority over the proceedings and charmed the audience, who in turn loved him. 'Not only by his production talent has he achieved greatness, but by the big-heartedness, the simple kindliness and staunch friendship which has always been part of his make-up.' During the Second World War he was in sole charge, producing the 1940/1 performance under great difficulties during the Blitz. In 1973 he retired aged ninety and died in 1979 aged ninety-seven. His name is remembered in Lockhart Close on the housing estate now built on the Belle Vue site.

The programme cover for the 39th circus at Belle Vue in 1967/8. That year George Lockhart celebrated his eighty-seventh birthday and eighty years in the circus. The season was called the 'George Lockhart Celebration Circus' in his honour. George's bandmaster was constantly Fred Bonelli, who had begun as a circus conductor forty years earlier. As a boy of nine, Fred, perched on top of a pile of books, had played trumpet with Barnum and Bailey's band. This 39th season included Antoine's black bears, Monsieur Flick the Indiarubber man, a diving tiger, Smart's twelve stallions, John Gindl's mighty elephants, Chipperfield's leopards and panthers and Equestriana.

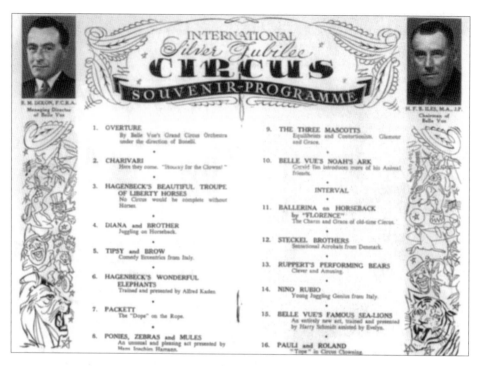

The programme for the Silver Jubilee of Belle Vue International Circus in 1953/4. John Henry Iles retired in 1937 and his son became chairman. Reginald Dixon was managing director from 1947 until 1956. The post-war boom had brought popularity again to Belle Vue and to its circus. Belle Vue's Noah's Ark was a novelty act tried out in the early 1950s by Gerald Iles. Zoo animals were brought in as circus acts, including the sea-lions, trained by the Schmidts.

Patricia Clark, the Belle Vue Railway Queen, visits members of the circus in 1932. Each year a Railway Queen was crowned (see p. 101).

Evelyn Schmidt and her performing dog at Belle Vue Circus in the 1950s. Evelyn was more usually seen with her husband 'Captain' Harry Schmidt and their Californian sea-lions. There were various acts of performing dogs over the years including 'Stephenson's famous acrobatic and football dogs' (1950s), 'Dubsky's wonderful football bulldogs' (1960s) and 'Phyllis Allan's poodles' (1970s).

The grand finale parade of all the stars of the Belle Vue Circus in the late 1970s. On the right is the ringmaster Norman Barrett, who presided over the ring from 1972 until 1981. Before him Roberto Germain, Yasmine Smart and Chris Christian had followed in George Lockhart's footsteps. Norman had the sad task of seeing a still popular circus perform for the 53rd and last time in the Kings' Hall at Christmas 1981. The circus did in fact continue on other sites until Christmas 1985/6. There were 'acts from all over the world, a wonderful atmosphere, a magnet. Conditions were good and there was a friendly and relaxed atmosphere.'

Left: A page from the Silver Jubilee programme for the 1953/4 circus season. Early programmes cost 2d or 3d. Through the 1950s and 1960s they maintained the price of 1d, rising to 1/6d or later 7½d in the 1970s. The final programme cost 25p. For 1953, 'Mr Dixon journeyed to the Continent to eventually cover many thousands of miles and view for himself the great artistry provided by the ring stars of some twenty leading circuses'. The only acts he could not bring back were the high wire or trapeze ones, as the roof of the Kings' Hall was not high enough.

Below: Director Gerald Iles (centre) with Matt Kelly (first on the right) and other keepers, with the animals he brought in as circus acts in the early 1950s. One act was called Noah's Ark. Here on the left are Evelyn 'Erna' and 'Captain' Harry Schmidt with their Californian sea-lions. The goat cart was also used in the zoo to give rides. The camels and reptiles came from the zoo.

Another view of Gerald Iles, with keepers and zoo animals used in the circus in the early 1950s. Here the camels are more visible, as are the chimpanzee, monkey and Ankola cow. 'Here's the special spot for young and old alike, a grand parade of Belle Vue's own zoo animals including snakes, monkeys, llamas, crocodiles, camels, lion cubs. Gerald Iles will introduce them and compère the act in his inimitable way, just as he has done, and still does, in his *Children's Hour* broadcasts.'

In the setting of the Kings' Hall polar bears perform their act in the 1960s.

The turn of the lions and tigers in the Kings' Hall in the 1970s. Over the years tigers, panthers and leopards had all performed within the caged area, as well as lionesses, elephants and polar bears. In the later years there were fewer performing animals and more human acts.

Evelyn and 'Captain' Harry Schmidt with their performing sea-lions in the circus arena of the 1950s. The Schmidts, or Smiths as they were earlier called, also trained their sea-lions to give shows at the pool in the zoo. Here each stand bears the name of its sea-lion: Peter, Freddy, Bisto and Berry. These displays lasted from 1948 until 1953.

' "Quaver and Semi-quaver", a Nocturne. Kindest regards from Lofty', reads the back
of this photograph from the 1940s. Clowns always formed an important part of Belle
Vue Circus. Back in the early 1950s there were 'Toby, La Fay and Stump, Tambo and
Tambo, August and Tempo and Ross and Willie, burbling with bubbling craziness, as
they tumble and jumble hither and thither to start the show.' In the 1960s there were
Len, Alby, Noe Noe, Ross Adam and Johnco. In the 1970s until closure, there were
Jacko Fossett and Little Billie. Jacko was with the circus for over thirty years.

Members of the circus in the 1940s.

A christening in the big top of the Kings' Hall in 1981. It was a Belle Vue tradition to hold an event like this for a circus family occasion. Here the performers and their families are lined up for the service, including, on the right, the ringmaster Norman Barrett and clown Jacko Fossett.

Jacko Fossett and the Revd Anthony Carr with the baby to be christened, in 1981. It is ironic that the last performance of the circus in the Kings' Hall should have been accompanied by the christening of a baby, a symbol of new life.

Five

The Amusements

The Amusement Park at Belle Vue in the 1950s. The Jennisons had set out a small amusements area to the left of the main Hyde Road entrance from the 1870s, between the Great Lake, the Indian Grotto and Lion House. It comprised steam-driven attractions: the Velocipedes (bicycles), horses, the Ocean Wave and the Jungle Shooting Range. In 1924 John Henry Iles set out, behind the old Jennison brewery, another new park, which eventually boasted of being 'the largest inland in the United Kingdom'. The famous 'Bobs' dominate the background and in the foreground (right), is the Caterpillar ride and the Kings' Hall. The Octopus is on the left.

Left: The children's playground before 1964, 'full of amusements for little folks'. The helter skelter, in the background, cost 6d a go. In the early 1900s there had been a helter skelter lighthouse on the banks of the Firework Lake.

Below: Baby cars in the Autodrome in the children's playground in the 1960s were advertised as 'cars just like daddy's'. In 1931 this area was added for small children, behind the King's Hall and sensibly near to the zoo shop and the Lost Children office. '"Safety First" has been the motto of the directors and here the kiddies will find the moments pass all too quickly while they revel in the attractions provided. Here are the usual big rides of the amusement park in miniature form.' In the background is the miniature train *Pioneer*.

Above: Queuing for the 'Hall of Laughter', in the 1950s, opposite the King's Hall. 'Laughter Land' was first introduced in 1908 as a hall of mirrors. It lay on the banks of the Firework Lake near the Waterfowl Lake and the helter skelter. The Pagoda marked its entrance. An amusement arcade was added later.

Right: Children enjoying the Whirly Bugs ride, while attending a schools' sports day in July 1946. See-saws, overboats, roundabouts and donkey rides were all part of the fun. Children from the orphanage came to Belle Vue on a special day out and they would walk around hand in hand and have free goes on the rides.

The miniature railway's *Railway Queen* in 1947. From 1928 until 1977 this popular railway operated on various circuits around Belle Vue. First it ran from the Longsight entrance along the tree-lined walk to the King's Hall (Parkside station). In 1936 the track was extended and a tunnel added. In 1957 it was relocated to run from the Great Lake to the ballroom, where there was a new station. Relocated again, in 1964, around the Firework Lake and the big cats enclosure and renamed the 'Santa Fe Railway', it acquired American-style features. By 1971, now known as the 'Belle Vue Steam Railway', it was little used. Other engines were called *King George V*, *Prince Charles* and *Joan*.

Crowds in the Amusement Park in the early 1950s. The Moonrocket ride is in the background with, probably, the 'Jack and Jill' on the right. In 1924-5 John Henry Iles provided the Flying Sea-planes, Caterpillar, Whirlpool, Whip, Jack and Jill, Hey-Day and Dodgem rides. More were soon added, such as the River Caves, Auto Scooter, Ghost Train, Miniature Brooklands, Scenic Railway, Bug and Whirlwind Racer.

The Amusement Park after its reopening during the war in 1943. It was packed full, with record crowds in 1944 and 1945. In the background lies the Bobs, with people queuing to the entrance on the right, probably the most famous landmark of Belle Vue. 'For the thrill of your lifetime have a ride on the Bobs Coaster.' 'This gigantic whirl is the first and the only one in Europe. Visitors have the unique opportunity of experiencing such a thrilling rush through space that would be the envy of a Malcolm Campbell.'

The construction of the Bobs in the 1920s. This 60 mile per hour, 80 feet high coaster opened in 1929 as a second scenic railway. John Henry Iles had it brought from the Wembley Exhibition in London, paying its American owner £20,000. The name 'Bobs' came from the price of a ride: 1s, to travel a mile a minute. It had ten cars, which travelled down angles of 45 degrees.

Right: The men who built the Bobs in the 1920s. One of the workmen was the Jennison's chief joiner at Belle Vue, Sam Pickford. Tragically he died young and his children were brought up by John Jennison's son, James.

Below: Construction of the Bobs in the 1920s on the site of the old stable block at the Hyde Road entrance. This position was important, as the Bobs could be seen from the main Hyde Road by passers-by and thus attract them in.

Enjoying the Bobs in 1958. Whatever the year, whatever the person's age, everyone enjoyed the thrill of a ride on this coaster. Although still in the *Guinness Book of Records*, in 1971 it was demolished, as maintenance was too costly and demand was in decline. 'This bone rattling, hair-raising terror trip became such a firm favourite that when it was dismantled in 1971 it was sold piecemeal to souvenir hunters.'

Left: An art student, Vance Tutton, aged twenty, making his record-breaking ride on the Bobs in 1967. Vance became the World Roller Coaster Champion by riding for about twelve hours round 325 circuits. He chose to sit in the back seat, setting off in the dark, with a volunteer crew handing him sandwiches and drinks as he passed by the station. As he went round, he even managed to play a game of chess with a friend and he won! The worldwide publicity was good for him and for Belle Vue.

Below: Crowds in the Amusement Park in 1946. The Caterpillar was one of many popular rides, as was the Scenic Railway behind it. Installed by John Henry Iles in 1926, the Caterpillar became so popular during the war that another one was constructed in 1945 but it was never as popular as the first one, so soon the park was back to one. A cover came up over the riders as they were lifted up and down and jets of air blew on to them. The original Caterpillar continued until about 1970.

The Electric Speedway ride in the park in the 1940s. The Moonrocket lies to the right in the background and the sea-lion house is in the distance. 'The fun never ends in the new Amusement Park. Off the Coaster on to the nearly as exciting Scenic railway; then on to the mysterious River Caves; then a spot of 'Over the Falls' or the Figure Eight railway. Not to mention the Flying Seaplanes, which give an exhilarating sensation not to be described in words; the Giant Caterpillars, Whirling Bugs, tricky Auto-scooters, Baby Motors and all sorts of nerve-tickling devices. And then the games – and what games!'

Ella Retford, Madge Saunders and George Clarke enjoy a ride on the Scenic Railway in 1931.

Children queuing to board the Scenic Railway during a visit for the schools' sports day in July 1946. For 3d a thrilling ride could be had on this railway, viewing the gardens of Belle Vue from above.

Riding the Scenic Railway in the 1940s.

Riding on the Scenic Railway in the 1940s. The 1928 guidebook reads, 'The Scenic Railway dominates Belle Vue. To see it at dark or in darkness, its cliffs picked out with lights, its vast grey body raised like a mountain range above the sports of pygmies on the plain, is to miss a thrill in anticipation. It takes you emotionally, as well as physically, from the depths to the heights. It puts the wind up you, through you and round you.'

Bill Campbell and his party posing outside 'The Scooter' in the Amusement Park in August 1946.

Crowds in the Amusement Park in the late 1940s outside the Palace of Strange Girls and the Jump a Copper. In the background is the Bobs. In 1954 there was a record-setting crowd on Good Friday with 230,000 visitors to the amusements over the Easter weekend.

The finalists for Miss Great Britain enjoying the Scenic Railway in August 1966. The railway continued to thrill visitors until the 1970s. The rising cost of repairs and the eventual decline in the ride's popularity led to it falling into disuse after 1975 and it was demolished in 1980.

The Enchanted Garden at Belle Vue in the early 1960s. This was set out in 1956 and incorporated an elevated tree walk over illuminated features. It lay next to the Avenue near the Longsight entrance. By 1963 the garden had become dilapidated and was dismantled.

A family standing around the Belle Vue stocks in the late 1960s. Behind them is the Slot Palace. Here the stocks are just by the main entrance, adjoining the old Lion and Tiger House. A set of stocks were originally in front of the helter skelter near the Indian Grotto. The Slot Palace was a new amusement arcade opened in 1966. By this time the Amusement Park was in decline; demand was dropping and the opening hours were cut down. By 1979 the park was farmed out on a concessionary basis to Alf Wadbrooke and was open only at weekends. In 1980 the park was closed altogether, ending 110 years of amusements at Belle Vue.

Six

At the Zoo

The opening day of the Children's Zoo in 1955. Actress Frances Lederer, dressed as Bo Peep, leads children around the animals, accompanied by H.F.B. Iles, who is standing behind her. The following year he continued as chairman but under the control of the Forte company. This Children's Zoo was the dream of his cousin Gerald Iles, the zoo's director. At a cost of £15,000, a world of concrete, aluminium and plastic was created with pools and streams, next to the old fireworks workshop. Included as the largest feature was 'Willie the Whale', which was made of concrete, measured 32 feet in length and 8 feet in height and housed a small aquarium.

Above: James Craythorne with the skeleton of Maharajah, an Indian male elephant, in the Natural History Museum at Belle Vue in the early 1900s. Originally housed on the Firework Island, it was moved in 1850 to the upper floor of a building near the main entrance. After being at Belle Vue for ten years, Maharajah had died of pneumonia but his skeleton remained on display at the museum until that closed fifty-nine years later. In 1941 it was transferred to Manchester University's museum for a fee of £30.

Left: Lorenzo Lawrence, in about 1912, celebrating forty years as elephant keeper at Belle Vue, where he had come with Maharajah in 1872. John Jennison's son, James, paid £680 for eight-year-old Maharajah at the sale of 'Wombwell's Royal Number 1 Menagerie' at Edinburgh. The journey to Belle Vue became a legend. After Maharajah broke out of the horsebox before the journey, Lorenzo declared they would walk. They took ten days and a painting in Manchester City art gallery recalls the famous 'Disputed Toll', when the elephant is said to have forced his way through a toll gate without paying. There was also a band composition called 'Lorenzo' composed in the keeper's honour.

Lorenzo with an elephant (possibly Sally) in about 1900. The elephants gave rides, performed in the firework spectacles, in pageants or at Whit and May Day processions, pulled loads and helped in demolition work. Elephants from Belle Vue pulled the stone pillars for St Elisabeth's church at Reddish. In the background is the firework viewing stand. The elephant ride steps and platform, on the left, were sited here until 1957.

Phil Fernandez, in costume, with Alec Helsby (first right) and Matt Kelly (second right), with other keepers and elephant Annie holding a Union Jack with her trunk, in March 1950. They greeted Princess Margaret as she passed by the Hyde Road entrance on her way to lay the foundation stone of the new Free Trade Hall. Phil was Malayan and came to Belle Vue from the East with an Indian female elephant, Lil, in 1921. She died at Belle Vue aged fifty in 1947 but Phil worked on and he died in 1956. Annie died in 1952.

Above: Children queuing for the Jungle Express ride in the 1940s. 'So the famous team of "Phil and Lil" came into being, which must have given pleasure to tens, perhaps even hundreds, of thousands of children. Fernandez in his colourful robes was a very popular figure in the Gardens and he had many friends. Lil was one in a thousand. How many visitors she carried on her ample back during her twenty-six years at Belle Vue is anyone's guess but, as she took fourteen at a time (mostly children), it must have totalled a pretty astronomical figure.'

Left: Phil Fernandez with an elephant in the 1940s. There were other elephants over the years. Sally arrived in 1869 and worked with Maharajah. 'Nellie' worked with Lil and there were Judy, Betsy, Dinah, Mary, Martha, Annie, and Ram Kali with Ram Moti in the 1960s. Ellie May had to be put down when she became ill while being moved as the zoo closed down in 1979.

Above: Children enjoying a ride on the Belle Vue Stage Express drawn by miniature pony in 1967. Some of these children had participated in the production of the Oberammagau Passion play at Belle Vue that year (see p. 110). Goats, llamas and camels were also used to give rides.

Left: Maude, the tigon, 1932-1949. 'No more those lustrous eyes will answer to my call.' These were the picture and caption on director, Gerald Iles', Christmas card, sent, in 1949, from his home at Longsight Lodge on Redgate Lane. Maude, a cross between a Manchurian tiger and an African lioness, came to Belle Vue from Germany in 1936, together with her brother Kliou, at a cost of £325. They were among the first tigons to be seen in Britain. He died in 1941 of tuberculosis but she lived on until 1949. In 1957, another tigon 'Rita' came to Belle Vue and died in 1968.

The gibbon cage in the late 1930s. To celebrate Belle Vue's centenary in 1936, Centenary Gardens were laid out near the main entrance, together with this floral clock, which was two faced, electrically operated and topped by a statue of Buddha. This innovative cage housed sixteen gibbons, with swings, pool, ropes and tightrope. Beyond the cage is Monkey Mountain, made of artificial rock, surrounded by a water-filled trench which dispensed with the need for bars or cages. In 1957 this was replaced by the Monkeyrama, which was a pit filled with concrete pillars. The Elizabethan Complex is on the left with the Birdcage Walk.

The original monkey house in about 1900. All the cages had a theme; this one, built by Jennison in 1881, had a Moorish style. Inside was a great central cage with smaller cages along the sides. The monkeys had for amusement a village pump and well for drawing water, an elevator for drawing corn, a large wheel, a rocking horse and gym equipment. This house remained intact until its redesign in 1958. In 1963 a Great Ape House was opened. On the left is the Small Waterfowl Lake, which existed until about 1925.

'Consul the Great, the almost man', in the late 1890s. There were two chimpanzees named Consul. 'Consul I' came to Belle Vue in 1893 but died in 1894, aged about five. His popularity was assured. A second chimpanzee was bought and named 'Consul II'. His party piece was to ride a tricycle, later a bicycle, while playing a violin.

Left: A memorial sheet to Consul 1, sold at a penny a time in 1894. Consul became a popular figure; dressed in a smoking jacket and cap and smoking a pipe, he would join James Jennison at business meetings. In later years there were other trained chimpanzees, such as Joey, who boxed in gloves, and Joan who was able to untie shoelaces.

Below: Keepers taking two young, dressed-up chimpanzees and an orang-utan (centre) for a walk in the 1900s. In the background is the monkey terrace, which was added to the side of the elephant house in 1890. It was quite common for keepers to take the monkeys for walks and in 1963 tea parties were put on for visitors' entertainment. 'One story my father [head gardener] told me: an orang-utan, or some monkey, escaped and it was found sat on the toilet. There were one or two houses in Belle Vue you know, up Kirkmanshulme Lane and inside Belle Vue itself. This monkey was there, that's where it was.'

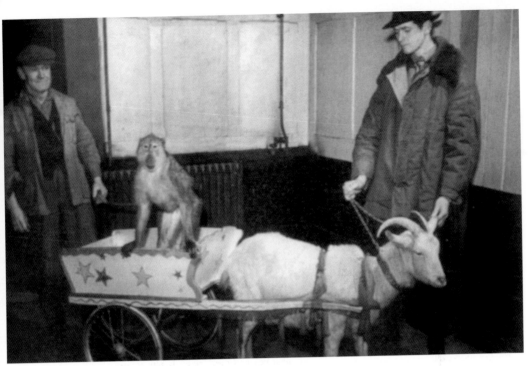

A goat pulling a cart and a monkey in the 1940s. Animals giving rides were always popular with children.

'Big snake cage. George Craythome [left] a fine poacher [of snakes] and snake keeper', George Jennison wrote on the back of this photograph in the early 1900s. Generations of the Craythorne family worked at Belle Vue. George cared for the live reptiles in the museum. His son James (seen earlier with the elephant skeleton) was employed for sixty-four years, until 1944, and cared for various types of animal, including sea-lions, parrots and reptiles. His son Albert followed in his footsteps. James was the first to breed the Indian cobra in England in 1931 and Clive Bennett the first to successfully breed a Royal Python in 1972. The reptiles were first housed in a tropical hot house together with plants and also in a tank in the Indian Grotto.

Keepers with camels and a zebu in the early 1900s. The Paddock Range with a pool, and later an enclosed paddock house with a central aisle with cages on either side, was built by Jennison in 1853. This housed an aviary at one end and animals such as deer, bison, sheep, goats, antelopes, llamas, Shetland ponies and kangaroos. In 1958 Gerald Iles' idea of a new ruminant enclosure near the children's zoo was put into practice. These had a surrounding wall and dry moat with timber-woven fenced areas for the animals.

'An enclosure with ornamental rockwork for mountain-living species, containing male Barbary sheep from the Atlas mountains in Morocco, Indian goats and Morocco rams' in the early 1900s built by the Jennisons in 1897. On the left lies the camel, giraffe and rhino house and the lamp on the right lay in the centre of the 'New Maze', opened in 1870. In 1928, a new Rocky Mountain enclosure was opened, next to the Paddock House. Constructed of artificial stone with a large pool and fountain, it housed Corsican Moufflon and Barbary Sheep.

Left: Admiring a giraffe in the 1950s. In 1871 four giraffes arrived at Belle Vue and in 1878 a small glass giraffe house was opened near Paddock Range. The early days were not very successful, until Gerald Iles took over. His first giraffe, Willie, was purchased by and named after his father, William. In 1938 the giraffes George and Mary produced a baby, which was named Doreen, and who remained there until the 1950s. Another camel family was Youki and Diana and their calf, Toby.

Below: A party outside the camel enclosure in the 1960s. The camels, like the elephants, llamas and goats, gave rides to children. They pulled six to eight children in an ingenious chariot. 'A camel ride is an unique sensation.' The Camel House, built in 1881 near Paddock Range, housed the Bactrian (the two-humped) camel. Camels were successfully bred at Belle Vue in the early days in the 1890s. In later years, there were two camels called Moses and Lucy; Moses was the bossier and always arrived first for any titbits.

The Sea-lion and Aquatic Birds House, with a pool on the right, in the early 1900s. It was built in 1885, next to the Camel House, and by 1888 it included a large indoor pool for displays which was sixty-four feet long, twenty feet wide and three feet deep. There was a stage and seating for several hundred people. The first keeper in charge of indoor pool displays was Jack Cupitt. 'The animals go through a variety of evolutions in the tank, diving from a height, leaping over poles, through hoops, swinging on the cross bars etc. The speed at which they rush through the water is most remarkable. The male sea-lions utter a loud barking noise.'

Visitors waiting for the feeding display at the outdoor sea-lion pool, in the late 1950s. Behind them the camels watch too from their outside enclosure. In 1899 'the visitor perceives an open-air tank, completed this season, for sea-lions and aquatic birds. The animals can pass to and from the large sea-lion house.' Here visitors were able to watch the sea-lions waddling out and feeding. The pool, which lay behind this building, was filled in after the Second World War.

Keeper Jack Cupitt with a sea-lion on a bench in the gardens in the early 1900s.

Evelyn 'Erna' and 'Captain' Harry with their performing Californian sea-lions in the early 1950s. After the Second World War, the Schmidts reintroduced sea-lions to the zoo. These displays were put on in the indoor pool, as by this time the open-air one had been filled in.

Above: 'Captain' Harry with his sea-lions performing in the indoor pool in the early 1950s. These included Bisto, Freddy, Ricardo, Peter, Asti and Berry. Ricardo would rest 'his chin momentarily on the edge of the pool before throwing himself backwards into the water to make another circuit, which would bring him back again to his resting point. Like the bear, the sea-lion would repeat his routine for very considerable periods of time.'

Left: Evelyn 'Erna' Schmidt on the right and Elizabeth 'Lil' Smith on the left, in the early 1960s, by the Paddock Range. Elizabeth worked as cashier for the sea-lion show for many years and was cashier at the Longsight and Hyde Road gates, the cloakroom and various rides. After sixteen years at Belle Vue, she retired in the late 1970s. Evelyn continued to look after the sea-lions after her husband, 'Captain' Harry's, death. She lived in a caravan on the site, as did many zoo keepers at Belle Vue.

'Captain' George Wilburn with his performing sea-lions in the 1970s. George took over from his grandfather and the displays continued. George wore a navy-style captain's cap for the performances.

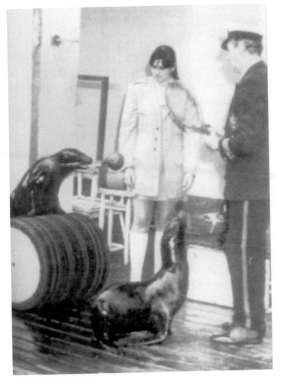

Christine Wilburn helping her father George with the sea-lion display in the 1970s George retired in 1975 and died in 1987 aged sixty-nine. His place was taken by 'Captain' Bill Burgess.

Sea-lions being fed by the outside pool in the early 1900s. By 1899 James Graythorne was in charge. Sea-lions were a favourite with visitors. One sea-lion could even play *God Save the King* by pushing its nose against the soft rubber bulbs of a set of motor horns arranged in a scale. In 1931, one sea-lion, Sarah, 'has lived in the gardens for eighteen years, and has a most consistent bark, which can be heard for quite a distance. For her regularity, she has been designated the knocker-up of Longsight'.

The pelicans on show in the Birds of Prey Terrace in the early 1900s. By the 1930s they had their own enclosure. In 1959 the old Monkey Terrace, on the side of the Elephant House, became the Birdcage Walk and in 1962 a second walk replaced this Birds of Prey Terrace, along the side of the Camel and Giraffe House. The pelicans were fed daily at tea-time in front of visitors.

A keeper with parrots in the early 1900s. An aviary was attached to the Paddock House, where parrots and smaller exotic birds were kept. In 1948, Gerald Iles created there the 'Hall of Living Jewels', housing exotic and brightly coloured small birds, such as humming-birds and birds of paradise and with a darkened viewing corridor for visitors. It consisted of a row of eleven glass-fronted cages. In 1969 the old aviary became home to a model railway.

The Pheasantry and Penguin House in about 1900. Built in 1888, it contained a forty-feet long glass tank. In 1930 it was briefly converted to a fresh water aquarium, until the penguins were introduced in 1933. By 1947 they were moved outside to a new pool in the Rocky Mountain enclosure and then to a new Penguinarium in 1962. In front of the house can be seen here the Tree Island Pond, which was home to swans and ducks. In 1962 it was improved and gained a mock Far Eastern-style pagoda and a new Pheasantry was opened in 1961.

The bear pits and polar bear cage in about 1900. Completed by Jennison in 1855 and then modernized by Gerald Iles in 1938, they were in use right up until 1960. Then new bear terraces were built at the back of the Firework Island with rocks and pools, walled by a moat and facing Kirkmanshulme Lane. The bears slept under the Firework Island picture in centrally heated cages. Other breeds were then added to the original brown and polar bears. The old cage here was later used as a lion enclosure but otherwise the pits lay derelict until demolition in 1964.

Seven

Eating and Drinking

The Chinese Café in about 1900. The Jennisons had themed areas and high-class restaurants like this, as well as cafés and areas for self-catering. This restaurant, formed from two of the larger tea-rooms in the ballroom block, was decorated in the Chinese style in 1889 and bear terraces refurbished in 1904. The walls had Chinese paintings, parasols shaded the tables and Chinese lanterns hung from the ceiling. By 1931 it could seat 150 people. Most of the catering staff were local people, 'I lived at Crossley Street, off Gorton Lane. It was a Belle Vue house. They had hundreds working there from all around Gorton. Our next-door neighbour was in charge of the Chinese restaurant, Mrs Ford' [1920s].

Tables set ready for use in the Hyde Road restaurant at Belle Vue in the 1930s. The formal style of the Edwardian era is still present, with potted palms, umbrella stands and a stag's head over the fireplace. This restaurant was situated at the main entrance. Originally it was an inn, 'the Belle Vue house', becoming the Hyde Road hotel and restaurant in 1925 and then the Palm Court in 1942.

The American Bar, seen here in the 1940s was destroyed by fire in 1958. There were also the Popular Restaurant in the ballroom block (destroyed in 1958), the Fish and Grill Restaurant (1928-1946) behind the 'firework picture', the Jolly Buffet Bar (demolished in 1963) by the giraffe house, the Maze Cottage refreshment room (1870s) and the Pagoda (up to 1957) to mention just some of the cafés of the early years. The 1892 guidebook boasts that also 'visitors, who have provided themselves with their own refreshments, may obtain hot water, teapots, cups, knives and other requisites, in the large new room, at the lower end of the Music Hall.' The charge was 2d each.

Mrs Phipps in the Tudor Bar in 1946. This lay under the firework stand and together with the Tudor Restaurant serviced the ballroom block. The area was created in 1936 from the old roller skating rink. The Tudor Room was destroyed, together with the Coronation Ballroom, in the fire of 1958.

The central bar of the Tudor Room in the 1940s. The theme was baronial with stags' heads, tapestry-style paintings, stained glass, barrels of beer and a timber-framing effect on the walls. The suite 'is tastefully furnished and decorated in the Old English style and is a particularly pleasant venue for party meals.'

Waiting to serve at a Masonic dinner in the Tudor Restaurant in the 1940s. Belle Vue 'has its own kitchens, bakeries, ice-cream factory and so on, and everything is freshly made daily.' The Jennisons had run a bakery, butchery, kitchen gardens and even an ice-making facility. Jennison flooded the fields in winter, cut out the ice and stored it in sealed 'great underground chambers'. In summer, the ice was 'crushed and mixed with flavouring and sold in the gardens as 'water ices'. He also 'maintained a dairy with herds of cattle, sheep and other livestock on the fields surrounding the zoo.'

Waitresses ready to serve at a Masonic dinner in the Chinese Restaurant in the 1940s. In 1931 Belle Vue boasted 'that the grounds offer every imaginable facility, from the humble penny-in-the-slot machine to the sweets kiosk, from cafés and tea-rooms to hot-water rooms for those who prefer to bring their own supplies, and so on, right up to first-class hotel catering.' A 1931 advertisement boasted that 'you can rely completely on the fare you get at Belle Vue, whether it be an ice-cream wafer or a seven-course dinner. Belle Vue has been entrusted with some of the largest catering contracts in Lancashire history, including CWS dinners for 1,250 persons – a testimonial which needs no stressing.'

Waitresses in costume at a theatrical ball in the Tudor Restaurant and bar in 1944. The theme is international, perhaps in a wartime show of solidarity.

A children's circus party from the General Company of Oldham in the 1940s. Mr Lilley organised the firm's treat of a circus outing and meal for the employees' families.

Another children's party in 1948. Belle Vue put on many such parties for children and also for wounded soldiers, evacuees and veterans during and just after the war, when treats were scarce.

Families at the same party as above in 1948.

The Ford Company's party in January 1945 for employees' families. Mr Hazelden, the work's manager at Ford's, is seen here talking to some of the children. The Ford Motor Company used Belle Vue to hold their own motor show from the early 1930s onwards. Many firms, as well as private parties such as weddings and christenings, used Belle Vue's catering facilities and ballrooms.

Ford's party in January 1945. Here wounded soldiers enjoy the occasion in the Tudor Bar in the ballroom block. The Tudor Restaurant and the Second Tea-room were also used for this very large party.

Tables laid out ready in the Tudor Restaurant in 1948. The occasion was a dinner for long-service employees from ICI.

A wedding party in the Palm Court Restaurant in the late 1940s. After the fire of 1958 destroyed the catering facilities of the ballroom block, this restaurant was extended to meet the need. In 1969 it was extended again and converted into Caesar's Palace, which included a Golden Fry Griddle Restaurant.

Tables set ready for a dinner dance in the Coronation Ballroom complex in the 1950s. The stage is set for the band and the balloons are at the ready.

The Baronial Hall in 1953; this too was destroyed in the fire of 1958. There was also a Bavaria Banqueting Suite, set to the right of the main entrance near the ballroom. In 1957, this was the first of the new themed catering outlets of the Fortes period which concentrated on the catering side. They had managed 50 functions in 1956 and 160 in 1957. Although the fire of 1958 destroyed much of the catering facilities, they still managed to handle over 500 functions in 1959.

Tables ready in the Palm Court Restaurant in the 1950s. The formality of this restaurant had continued from the 1940s.

The bar of the Carlisle Lounge in the late 1950s. Before the 1958 fire there were also York and American Bars. From 1959 the new Edinburgh suite in the New Elizabethan complex contained the Carlisle Lounge, the York and Crystal Bars and the Fountain Lounge. The latter had a dancing water display activated by music. The Edinburgh Room had six Scottish murals designed by Syd Lane.

The Mexican Bar of the Kendal Banqueting Suite with South American motifs, 1960s. After the fire of 1964, this suite was added to those of the Cumberland and Windermere, so that all three together could cater for 1,500 people. It claimed to be 'the largest banqueting area outside London'. Each suite had its own sprung dance floor and stage. There were moveable, soundproofed screens to alter the size of each suite and to make them independent of each other.

The Lighthouse Café and bar by the Firework Lake in the 1950s, with the Indian Grotto on the left. In 1863 there were seven refreshment rooms seating from 100 up to 1,000. By the 1930s there were fifteen catering outlets: the Imperial, Japanese, Princess, First, Emperor and Gallery tea-rooms, plus the Chinese, First Class and Oriental cafés, the Hyde Road and Fish and Grill restaurants, the Exhibition Hall restaurant and the Hot Water Room, as well as the Club and Dining Rooms and the ballroom. On the left in this picture is the Reptile House.

The Lighthouse Café by the Firework Lake in the 1960s. This was refurbished and extended in 1958, as was the nearby Top Lake refreshment room by the renamed Great Lake. Originally the Lighthouse was opened in 1862 by the Jennisons as a 'spacious and lofty refreshment room', catering for 1,000. In 1977 it closed down as a bar, having already ceased to function as a restaurant. Prices in 1892 included tea or coffee 3d, ginger beer 2d a bottle, champagne 10s a bottle, bitter ale 2½d a glass and cigars 2d or 3d.

Tables set for 2,560 diners from the firm of W.J. Glover Ltd, in the Cumberland Suite in 1968. This suite had the best catering facilities, servicing dinner dances and also beer festivals. It started life as the Exhibition and Belfast Hall restaurants and, after the 1958 fire, was rebuilt as this suite, together with another one called the Windermere. Another fire ravaged it in 1964. Again it was rebuilt but as a bar with Victorian bric-a-brac and brassware. The Windermere became a bar with a nautical theme.

A dinner dance in a banqueting suite in 1965.

An advertisement for Caesar's Palace at the main entrance in 1975. Beginning as an inn, 'the Belle Vue house' and then becoming the Hyde Road Hotel and Restaurant in 1925, it was renamed the Palm Court Restaurant in 1942. It was extended and turned into Caesar's Palace in 1969, containing the Golden Fry Restaurant and a cabaret bar.

The exterior of Caesar's Palace in the early 1970s. In 1976 it became Jennison's Ale House and the restaurant became an amusement arcade. It finally closed in 1980 after some of the façade fell down.

Left: An advertisement for Caesar's Palace in 1971 with 'Ancient Rome' as its theme. There had been a hotel at each entrance in the Jennison era. 'Belle Vue has three fully licensed hotels within its boundaries; the main entrance hotel, the lake entrance hotel and the Longsight entrance hotel. All three are modern, comfortable and well managed, and offer a hearty welcome.'

Below: The Longsight Hotel on Redgate Lane, west of Hunter's Lane, in the 1960s. It was originally part of the entrance, built in 1851, together with a ballroom above the entrance. The hotel was demolished in 1985 and the new Longsight public house was built on Kirkmanshulme Lane.

An advertisement for the Lake Hotel, Hyde Road, in 1975. Built in 1876 with free stabling for visitors to Belle Vue, it was extended in 1929. In 1960 it was extended again with the Lake Room for concerts and the smaller Gloucester Room. It closed down in the 1980s and was demolished. Many public houses outside the site served visitors to Belle Vue, including the Midland Hotel, Three Arrows, Victoria, Rock Inn, Cheshire Hunt and Coach and Horses.

The remains of Jennisons' brewery in the 1980s. From 1872 the Jennisons brewed their own beer and ginger beer and also made lemonade, in a brewery near Hyde Road. There were 5,000 barrels in a honey-combed cellar linking the Music Hall with the Hyde Road entrance. The brewery was closed in 1928.

Eight

VIPs and
Special Events

Colonel 'Buffalo Bill' Cody with the Indians of his Wild West show on a tram outside 'the Belle Vue House' inn at the entrance to Belle Vue in 1903. William Cody was an army scout during the Sioux wars in the Wild West in America. He killed 4,820 buffalo in eighteen months, so gaining his nickname. From 1883 he toured America and Europe with this Wild West Show, which included Chief Sitting Bull and Annie Oakley. Buffalo Bill, who is standing here at the top of the tram steps, died in 1917. The company appeared at Brooks's Bar Park and was on a day trip to Belle Vue.

Left: George Danson in the late 1800s. He and his sons were London-based scenic artists of theatrical screen painting. The Jennisons brought them to Manchester and every year from 1852 until 1894 they designed and painted a new 'picture', which was set up on Firework Island and formed the backdrop to the fireworks spectacles. 'There was the fireworks island and also the "firework shop", where the various set-pieces and rockets were made. The two powder magazines still had gunpowder stored in them' [in 1928]. James Jennison directed this factory, which lay inside the perimeter wall near Kirkmanshulme Lane and was later moved to the old swimming pool site.

Below: The firework spectacle on Firework Island with spectators visible in the foreground, 1940s. The first 'picture' in 1852 was about 30,000 square feet in size and was the backdrop for 25 men with 300 rockets, 25 large shells and 50 Roman Candles, who re-enacted 'the Bombardment of Algiers', watched by 18,000 people. Each guidebook gave detailed historical notes about the battle portrayed that year. Up to the Second World War, a professional soldier, Sergeant Branwell, was in charge of the displays. He drilled his 'soldiers', many of whom were ex-servicemen, carrying weapons with bayonets in place.

The cover of the 1892 guidebook, advertising Dansons' great open-air picture of Cape St Vincent. From 1852 until 1969 firework displays were the highlight of the year at Belle Vue. Earlier in 1842 'splendid fireworks were exhibited at Belle Vue by Signor Pietro [Mr Richardson] of the Chapel House Gorton'. In 1846 there was a 'dissolving diorama' of fireworks by Francklin and Carroll of London. The Dansons took over in 1852 when the first 'Painted Picture' was created.

One of the famous Belle Vue 'Guys' outside the main entrance in the 1950s. Each year, from the 1930s until the 1950s, a 'Guy' advertised the firework spectacle, which was premiered at Whitsun and usually performed during August and on special occasions. The First World War did not stop the event: they just left out the rockets. Coronation Year in 1937 saw the spectacle of 'the Golden Pagoda of Rangoon'. The shows stopped for the period 1940 to 1945. Post-war, battle scenes with actors were dropped initially but by popular demand they were brought back by 1955. The firework viewing area was capable of holding 4,000 spectators but was lost in the 1958 fire. The remaining rubble was used to raise up the island to compensate for the loss of height on land.

Zoological Gardens,
BELLE VUE.

DINNER

TO THE

Crimean Infantry Veterans

ON

Thursday, September 20th, 1894.

ALMA DAY.

THE RIGHT HON. THE LORD MAYOR OF MANCHESTER

WILL PRESIDE.

The cover of the menu for the dinner held at Belle Vue in 1894 in honour of the infantry veterans of the Crimean War. Held appropriately on Alma Day, in memory of that battle, this dinner was attended not only by the Lord Mayor of Manchester but also by Ben Brierley, a local dialect poet, who had written a famous poem immortalizing 'Daisy Nook' during that war. As the crowd cheered his arrival, he said 'they thowt I was one of 'em' [a veteran] as he passed in to the dinner. The band of the King's Liverpool Regiment played a programme of music, including *Death of Nelson*, *Dear Home-Land*, *Voyage in a Troopship* and *The Relief*.

Leonard Williams, head gardener, with the Belle Vue Railway Queen, planting a tree in the gardens in about 1928. 'That tree was planted in the part that goes up to Longsight, I think, where there's an exhibition hall.' From 1925 up until 1970, with a break during the war, a Railway Queen was crowned in the King's Hall at the annual railway carnival. 'Chosen from railway employees' daughters, she represented peace and goodwill between railwaymen at home and abroad'.

Left: The war memorial to Belle Vue employees who died in action during the First World War. This memorial was unveiled by Angelo Jennison in Gorton public cemetery in November 1926 at a cost of £140 9s 4d. There were nineteen names, two of which were Jennisons. During that war, the company allowed the army to use part of Belle Vue at no cost. The Manchester Regiment drilled there; aircraft parts were manufactured as well as munitions. Many of the zoo keepers and other staff volunteered for action. The same pattern occurred during the Second World War.

Below: The Lancashire Cotton Pageant, held in the stadium at Belle Vue in 1932. This was the first in a five-year pageant plan at Belle Vue. Money was scarce, the cotton industry was in decline and so this pageant lost money badly and the plan was scrapped. Visually it was a success with its twelve episodes, ranging from 'a Persian market' through 'the Lancashire Witches, Lancashire play, work and at market' and ending with 'Lancashire Cotton for the World'. Finally 'King Cotton' rode in a triumphal car, dragged by 800 children and paid homage to by a cast of 12,000. There were 1,000 models dressed in Lancashire cotton and people of all nations accompanied him.

THE STADIUM, BELLE VUE, MANCHESTER

LANCASHIRE COTTON PAGEANT

President: Rt. Hon. THE EARL OF DERBY, K.G.

Under the auspices of
The Joint Committee of Cotton Trade Organisations.
Lancashire Industrial Development Council.
Manchester Development Committee.

12,000 Performers. Operatic Chorus of 1,500 voices. Ballet of 500. Four Brass Bands. Pageant Military Band of 60.

Evenings at 7-30 : Sat. June 25th to Sat. July 9th. Extra Performances at 3 p.m.
Sat. June 25th, Sat. July 2nd, Sat. July 9th.

Scenario by Matthew Anderson. Produced by Edward P. Genn.

Women Unionists visiting Belle Vue in 1932. This was a group from the Hollingworth branch of the Unionists. Many firms and social groups organised trips to Belle Vue's attractions or held annual or special dinner dances there.

Gorton's Rose Queen, Joan Barker, with the Belle Vue Golden Apple winner, Eva Withers, in 1932. Standing on the right is Mr 'Fatty' Banks, the Cotton King, who was part of the spectacle at the Cotton Pageant that year. As Belle Vue lies in the township of Gorton, it was appropriate that the town's Rose Queen should be present. The Golden Apple was a beauty contest run in conjunction with the Cotton Pageant.

Invitation card, inviting Mrs Ellen Williams to an Old Folks' Treat at the Exhibition Café in May 1935. The Lord Mayor of Manchester, Samuel Woollam, issued this invitation in honour of the Silver Jubilee of King George V and Queen Mary. On the reverse is written: 'On production of this ticket to the guard of a tramcar or 'bus, you will be conveyed to and from the place of the treat free of charge.'

Al 'Scarface' Capone's $20,000 bulletproof gangster car was on display at Belle Vue in the 1940s. It was stored afterwards in the stables at the rear of the Lake Hotel.

Dutch children carrying out a 'planting of the bulbs' ceremony at Belle Vue in September 1946.

The Church Lads' and Girls' Brigades at a rally in the stadium in July 1946. Behind lies the Amusement Park and the Scenic Railway. At one time the Lads' rally was held first and the Girls' in the week following.

Schoolchildren competing in Manchester schools' sports day in May 1947. From 1887, for twenty-five years, the athletic ground next to Hunter's Lane had been used for the annual Manchester and Salford schools' sports day. 'We all had new running pumps and would cheer our favourite teams. Mine was Ducie Avenue with their amber and black outfit with a golden bee embroidered on the front of the vest. How I longed to wear it! This sports day would wind up happily with us watching, across the lake, the firework display.' In 1929 the ground was turned into a speedway stadium and a new sports ground was opened near Redgate Lane. Here the sports day is held in the speedway stadium. The Scenic Railway is in the background.

Members of the Air Training Corps with a jet-engine in their hut at Belle Vue in the mid-1950s. They were based behind the Longsight Hotel near the Longsight entrance. Third from right is Alan Smith, whose mother Elizabeth 'Lil' Smith spent most of her life working at Belle Vue, especially as cashier at the sea-lion enclosure. The ATC also played football at Belle Vue (see page 120). In 1951 an RAE jet fighter cockpit was displayed at the Homes and Fashion exhibition at Belle Vue.

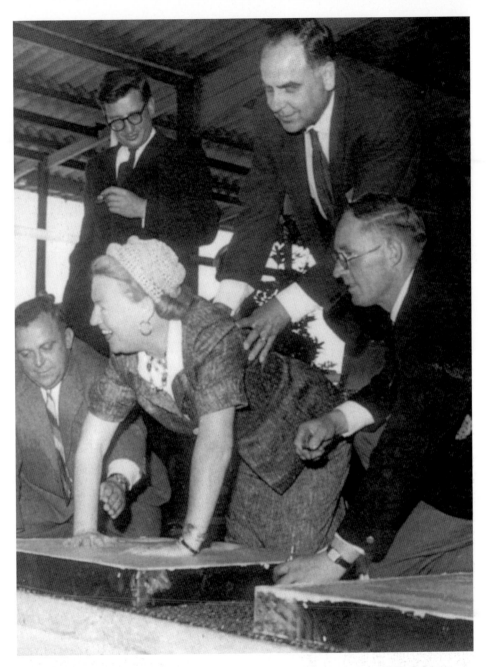

Gracie Fields imprinting her hands for the 'Wall of Fame' at Belle Vue in June 1959. Gracie was the first celebrity to have her feet and hands immortalized in concrete in the New Elizabethan complex, which replaced the old Coronation Ballroom destroyed by fire in 1958. The Wall of Fame was situated near the main entrance by Caesar's Palace. Gracie visited Belle Vue many times, especially the zoo. 'Gracie Fields accepted a gift of two dingo puppies. But she had to return them when neighbours complained of their serenades to the moon.' Other personalities who left their mark at the Wall of Fame included Pele, the footballer, Bing Crosby, Sir Winston Churchill and Sir John Barbirolli.

Queen Elizabeth II visited Belle Vue's speedway stadium in May 1961, to present the guidons or colours to the Duke of Lancaster's Own Yeomanry. Afterwards Her Majesty and her party were entertained in the Windermere suite. The parts of the gardens that lay on her route and the stadium were spruced up for the occasion.

An advertisement for 'Mini Land', Belle Vue's model village, in its opening year in 1966. Syd Lane, Belle Vue's scenic artist at that time, made and painted over 600 models to put in this village, which covered part of the old Paddock Field and the sports ground, next to the Ruminant Enclosure. Jimmy Clitheroe performed the opening ceremony of this £50,000 project. At night the village was all lit up and was described as 'the finest in Europe'. Models included a Cornish fishing village, a model railway and Ann Hathaway's cottage. It was closed in 1977 when Belle Vue itself closed down.

108

Above: Swedish folk dancers performing for the crowds in front of the 'Bobs' in 1966. There had been various folk festivals, including a folk dancing one, in 1952.

Left The comedian Ken Dodd and the Prime Minister Harold Wilson at Belle Vue stadium to celebrate the Labour Party Festival Day in the 1960s. With them is the North West Festival of Labour princess. Harold Wilson was entertained in the Vatican bar at Caesar's Palace. This was the directors' private bar and in this panelled room they had also welcomed Sir Winston Churchill, Sir Harold Macmillan and the Duke of Gloucester. Herbert Morrison made a speech at Belle Vue in 1950 and Sir Anthony Eden in 1957, both in the King's Hall.

Preparing for the performance of the Obergammau and Thiersee Passion Play at Belle Vue in February 1967. The actual performance proved controversial.

Resting during rehearsals for the Passion Play in February 1967. Numerous children were involved in the performance who also toured the zoo and Amusement Park, enjoying the rides (see p. 67).

A visitor from Russia being shown around Belle Vue in 1968. Behind them lies the 'Bobs' and on the right is the Bavaria Bier Halle. This was the first occasion that the Speedway Aces welcomed a Leningrad team. Here, from the left, are Morris Marshall, Sir Leslie Joseph, a Russian visitor and Michael Pickard of Forte.

An International Jazz festival in 1963. Jazz, rock and pop festivals and concerts were held regularly in the 1960s and 1970s. Fans massed to hear stars such as the Rolling Stones, Lulu, Tom Jones, The Hollies, Wayne Fontana, The Osmonds, Vera Lynn, Andy Williams, Annie Ross, Petula Clark, Johnnie Ray, Nat 'King' Cole and Doris Day. The Kings' Hall, or the suites, were used. In the 1960s a 'Rockarama' was staged in the Cumberland Suite with a stage at each end, used alternately by the groups, performing to over 1,000 fans.

A member of the Canadian Hell Drivers performing in the speedway stadium in the 1950s. Stock car racing was introduced from America by Johnnie Hoskins in 1954. It was a first for Belle Vue in the North West and proved very popular, with nine meetings a year and continuing until 1987.

Another stunt performed by the Canadian Hell Drivers in the stadium in the 1950s.

Nine

Sports, Halls
and ... the End

Ken Sharple (centre) and V. Parkiand, the winner of the garf race, with some of the other quarter-milers
and officials in June 1955. The garf race, which involved controlling a wheel with a stick, took place
in the speedway stadium. Ken began as a speedway rider and was team manager from 1960 until 1963,
taking over from Johnnie Hoskins. Johnnie had introduced speedway to Britain and Hoskins Close, on
the Belle Vue housing estate, is named after him. Johnnie succeeded Alice Hart, the only lady manager in
England, who in turn had succeeded the first manager E.O. Spence.

The speedway stadium in 1931. The original athletics ground of 1887, next to Hunter's Lane, turned into this speedway stadium in 1929 and was the first purpose-built track in Britain. Prior to that, in 1928, the greyhound stadium was used for speedway. The covered stands could hold 25,000 people with room for 40,000 overall. This stadium was used as well for many other events and sports, such as football, cricket, baseball, tattoos, pageants, rallies, car racing and tennis.

An action shot of riders on the 'Wall of Death' in July 1946. This was in the Amusement Park and involved motor bikes performing a gravity-defying ride. Tickets cost 1s. The structure was a round tub shape, lined with timber, and the motor bikes were ridden round the horizontal floor and then up and around the walls.'

Jack la Rue's party leaving the 'Wall of Death' in 1948. 'The rider came round with someone on his shoulders, came right to the top, as if it would come off. Everybody held their breath'.

Above: Belle Vue Speedway stars, champions of the Northern League, in 1929-1930. The 1930s saw these successes, coupled with national trophies. Back row from left to right: Wilf Mulliner, Max Grosskreutz, A.E. Simons, 'Acorn' Dobson, Oliver Langton, Arthur Franklyn, Eric Worswick. Middle row: B.L. Brook (track manager), J.M. Cockburn, Indian Allen, Len Blunt, E. Mangnall, F. Burgess, E. Young, George Hazard, Cyril Crowther, H. Bentley, Jack Harris (team manager). Front row: Tommy Simpson, Eric Langton, Bob Harrison, 'Curly', 'Johnny', Frank Varey, Walter Hull, Chun Moore and Dicky Fletcher.

Right: The programme cover for Belle Vue Aces in April 1960. Speedway, or dirt-track racing, was extremely popular at this time. The Aces were Belle Vue's own team and competed successfully against many other teams from at home and abroad, including Russia, Australia and Sweden. The Aces produced world champions, such as Peter Craven and Peter Collins. In the late 1960s they were Triple League champions. Even during the Second World War races were continued by using wood alcohol for fuel. The speedway trophy was shaped like a helmet and inscribed with the winner's name.

Watching a speedway race in the stadium in the 1970s. This was described as 'the greatest thrill of the age' in 'the finest speedway in the country with covered accommodation for 40,000 people: an all-star cast of riders.' The Aces were particularly successful and popular in the mid-1930s and then again in the 1960s. Supporters wore a club badge and were issued with a bar for each year of membership. In 1982, however, the stadium was sold to Stuart Bamforth. In spite of improvements and innovations, in 1987 he sold the site to a car auctions group. Peter Collins then set up the Aces in the greyhound stadium.

A soap box derby at Belle Vue in the early 1960s. Go-Kart racing was introduced by the speedway manager, Johnnie Hoskins, in 1959 but it proved unsuccessful. In 1954 he had also introduced 'Johnnie's Marching Girls', a group of thirteen girls, dressed in red and white, who paraded during speedway events.

'Doc' Garth receives his speed car trophy from a lady supporter, who was celebrating her twenty-first birthday, in the 1950s.

The greyhound stadium at the top of Kirkmanshuime Lane in 1990. The original stadium was the first to be built in the country. The Greyhound Association was formed in 1925 with Sir William Gentle of Belle Vue in charge. They leased the new £22,000 stadium from Belle Vue and here the first race in this country took place in July 1926. In 1937 the stadium was sold to Greyhound Racing Association with the provision that it must be used for greyhound racing and Belle Vue gave up control of the site.

LET'S ALL GO
TENPIN BOWLING

THE NORTH'S LEADING LUXURY CENTRE
IS RIGHT HERE

BELLE VUE
GRANADA BOWL

★ 32 Fully Automatic Lanes

★ League Meeting Room

★ Complete Catering

★ Kiddies Corner

★ Car Park

★ Licensed Bar

An advertisement for Tenpin Bowling at the Granada Bowl, in 1966. Up until 1963 the Top Lake, previously called the Great Lake, had occupied this corner of Belle Vue, on Hyde Road, behind the Lake Hotel. Granada Bowl was opened in 1965. It was a great success, having thirty-two automated lanes, a children's nursery and a club meeting room. When the rest of Belle Vue was sold off in 1981, bowling continued and the site was sold to First Leisure Group in 1983. A snooker club was opened in a corner of the car park in 1985, which still operates, and there is a bingo hall on the bowling site.

The Air Training Corps football team with their cups in May 1945. The speedway stadium was also used for football, baseball and rugby, on a grassed pitch in the centre of the speedway track. In 1931, invited by John Henry Iles, Manchester Central amateur football club came to Belle Vue and became 'a Mecca for football fans during the winter'. In fact they met with mixed success and in 1933 Broughton Rangers rugby football league club replaced them at Belle Vue.

Belle Vue Rangers play against Hull at rugby football in the speedway stadium in the 1950s. A twenty-one-year lease with £4,000 investment began rugby football at Belle Vue stadium in 1933, with the rental based on attendance figures. Belle Vue management had taken over the Broughton Rangers rugby league football club. After the Second World War play began again in 1945 with the team taking the name of Belle Vue Rangers. The venture proved a financial burden for Belle Vue and, when the lease ran out in 1955, the team was disbanded.

CHARITY MATCH

in aid of

The Alexian Brothers Nursing Home
Moston - Manchester 10.

Promoted by: Charles Mitten Esq.
Sponsored by: Messrs John Foy Esq.,
Gus Demmy Esq.

between-

Tommy Steele's
All-Star XI

Jack Crompton, Johnny Aston, Harry Greenaway,
Jimmy Scoular, Sid Owen, Henry Cockburn,
Tommy Steele, Joe Slone, Nat Lofthouse,
Stan Pearson, Charlie Mitten.

and . . .

Tommy Lawton's
All-Star XI

Colin McDonald, Brian Connerton, Wilf McGuiness,
Ron Burgess, Eddie Lowe, Don Revie, Roy Clarke,
Harold Hassell, Tommy Lawton, Jackie Milburn,
Brian Henry.

match played

Stadium - Belle Vue, Manchester

Sunday, August 4th 1963
Kick off 3-0 p.m.

SOUVENIR charity programme, price **2/6d**

ON SALE AT BELLE VUE

We would like to express our appreciation to the Directors of Belle Vue for their spontaneous co-operation.

A charity football match between Tommy Steele and Tommy Lawton All-Star XI teams in August 1963. Special matches, including charity events like this, were also held in the speedway stadium. This one raised funds for the Alexian Brothers' Nursing Home at Moston. The referee was K. Dagnall and the teams included footballers and jockeys.

A rally of the Union of Catholic Mothers in the Kings' Hall in April 1931. His Grace the Lord Archbishop of Liverpool and the Lord Bishop of Salford addressed the audience. The 1930s to the 1950s saw many such rallies in this hall. High tea and a variety concert or music and community singing often accompanied the rallies. At one rally in 1932, an incredible 4,000 'meat teas' were served. Converted from a tea-room in 1910 and enlarged in 1928, the hall could seat 7,000 people and was the venue for a wide variety of entertainments over the years.

An advertisement for wrestling at the Kings' Hall in 1966. The first contest took place in 1930 and proved to be very popular. Except for a break during the Second World War, the contests continued until 1981 and the end of Belle Vue's life. In the late 1930s Kathleen Look, wife of the speedway manager, E.O. Spence, presided at Belle Vue as the country's only woman promoter. A famous contestant at Belle Vue, from the 1940s to the 1960s, was Jack Pye.

Opposite: The cover of the souvenir programme for the Lightweight Championship contest of Great Britain between Frank Johnson (Manchester) and Joe Lucy in the King's Hall in April 1956. From 1929 until the Second World War, Belle Vue became 'the boxing Mecca of Europe'. In the 1930s Jackie Brown, Johnny King and Jock McAvoy were all British champions, Jackie Brown becoming World Champion in 1932. Post-war contests did not achieve the same peak of popularity, although a world championship fight was televised from Belle Vue in 1964 between Terry Downes and Willie Pastrano. Fire had just wrecked two of the banqueting suites and training facilities were set up in a fire-damaged kitchen with a ring on the tiled floor and emergency heating and lighting.

SOUVENIR OF A
FIFTEEN (3-min.) ROUNDS CONTEST at 9st. 9lbs. FOR THE LIGHTWEIGHT CHAMPIONSHIP
OF GREAT BRITAIN AND THE LORD LONSDALE CHALLENGE BELT
between

FRANK JOHNSON

(MANCHESTER) Holder, who has already registered two title wins (a third will make
the Lonsdale Belt his own property).

and

JOE LUCY

(MILE END) Challenger. Former Champion, who has a win over Johnson and recently
k.o.'d Gordon Goodman in a Final Eliminator.

FRIDAY, 13TH APRIL, 1956
KINGS HALL, BELLE VUE, MANCHESTER

OFFICIAL PROGRAMME   ONE SHILLING

The Kings' Hall set ready for 'Britain's biggest bingo bonanza', in the 1960s. In 1961 Belle Vue introduced bingo sessions to cater for this growing leisure activity. It was advertised as 'the largest bingo club in the country' with twice-weekly sessions on Fridays and Sundays. About 3,500 people attended each evening but by 1964 the Friday session had ceased, but the Sunday evenings continued until 1966.

T.W. Davey's stand at the Manchester Grocers' Exhibition in the Kings' Hall in 1936. This annual exhibition included a window dressing contest. In 1954 110,000 people visited it over the ten days. The exhibition hall also offered one of the largest display areas outside London. A huge hall, covering 100,000 square feet, it had its own large restaurant. In 1956 it was split off from the rest of the Belle Vue site and converted into three halls under one roof, so that three exhibitions could operate simultaneously. In 1987 it was sold to a car auction group, as alternative exhibition halls in Birmingham and Manchester became available.

A fire at Belle Vue in 1963. The symbol of an Ace can be seen on the speedway stadium on the left. In 1910 a fireman had died in a fire but amazingly the firework displays over the years had not caused major problems. Fire proved to be an expensive and ever-present hazard in the later years at Belle Vue. The most devastating fire was in 1958, when the Coronation Ballroom was destroyed, together with the York Bar, Tudor Suite, Baronial Hall, Popular Café, Pagoda Restaurant, staff canteen, six shops and the firework viewing stand.

Damage at the Longsight side of Belle Vue in October 1947. Vandalism and theft were also serious problems in the later years. In 1960, thirty-eight birds were killed one night by intruders. In that same year a sweets' kiosk and the Scooterland ride (the dodgems) were damaged by fire, causing £5,000 worth of damage. These and other such problems seemed to herald the end for Belle Vue, as they became progressively more frequent and serious.

Above: The House of Nonsense was destroyed by this fire in 1963, together with three other buildings. In 1964 the Windermere and Cumberland banqueting suites were destroyed by fire, which also engulfed the Ghost Train and the catering and laundry blocks. In 1969 yet another fire damaged the Ghost Train, for the second time, and also an amusement arcade.

Left: Demolition taking place in 1980. From 1977 onwards, after the closure of the zoo, Belle Vue was slowly taken apart, until only the greyhound stadium and Granada Bowl and snooker club were left.

Belle Vue in the process of demolition in 1983. Many of the public houses in the area closed down as well, as customers became scarcer.

The Kendal and Windermere banqueting suites lying empty and about to be demolished in 1988. 'I didn't go in the later parts because it was very upsetting to go after you've seen it in its glory. It should never have closed. It was such a beautiful place. It was like the forerunner of those theme parks. It was all there. It was right on the doorstep. Everybody came from all over. There was everything there.'

A party of schoolgirls queue to get into the circus in the early 1950s.

Acknowledgements

We acknowledge the help given by Dr Michael Powell and the staff at Chetham's Library and by the staff at the Local Studies Unit at Manchester Central Reference Library. We also acknowledge the research and publications produced by Robert Nicholls, Roy Nicol and Gerald Turner Iles. We thank the following people for allowing their memories to be included in this book: Margaret Hinde (daughter of head gardener Leonard Williams), Gerald Turner Iles, Leonard and Elizabeth Smith and Sir Jimmy Savile.

We should like to thank the following organisations and individuals for giving us permission for the use of their photographs in this book. We have tried to trace the origin of each photograph in the collection of Stan Horritt and we apologize if anyone has been omitted and not credited. We acknowledge Ashton Weekly Newspapers Ltd, the *Daily Mail*, the *Oldham Evening Chronicle* and the *Manchester Evening News*. Belle Vue publicity department employed the services of commercial photographers, whom we name but have been unable to trace:

Bertram Boor, Leo Carter, Ralph Frumin, Grove & Son & Boulton, Arthur Hamer, W.E. McClure, Mack & Co., John Madden, Thomas Mason, The Phoenix Studio, Thomas Renshaw, Shepherd Photographic Enterprises, J. Smart, John Spence, T.N. Studios, Warwick Picture Service & H. Bedford, Wright Wood.

Dr Michael Powell and Chetham's Library, Peter Clowes, Allan Crockford, Gina Dodd for the collection of the late Stan Horritt, Alice Hazelton for the collection of Evelyn Schmidt, Margaret Hinde, Mr McQuire, Robert Rhodes, Elizabeth and Leonard Smith, Cohn Southworth, Christine Wilburn and Mrs Wilburn.